I0622177

Contribitors

Pastor Dan Christiaans
Pastor Andrew McCombe
Jeyran Main
Ethan Davenport
Samantha Egan
Paul Van Kesteren
Jennie Marshall
Trent Kenney
Farmer Thomas Olsen
Effie Gabriel

MAPLE CITY BAPTIST CHURCH

LIVING IN LIGHT OF THE **CROSS**
MAGAZINE

Editor in Chief: S. Jeyran Main
Publisher: Review Tales Publishing & Editing Services
Cover Design: Samantha Egan
Designs: Pexels
ISBN 978-1-988680-48-4 Paperback
ISBN 978-1-988680-49-1 Digital
www.MapleCityBaptistChurch.com
For all inquiries please contact us directly.

LIVING IN LIGHT OF THE CROSS MAGAZINE
MAPLE CITY BAPTIST CHURCH

SSO GLAD
YOU'RE HERE!

Editor's Note

✝ = ♡

Welcome to the latest edition of "Living in Light of the Cross Magazine," a seasonal journey of faith brought to you by Maple City Baptist Church. In this issue, we embark on a thematic exploration of the book of Esther, delving into its timeless lessons and uncovering how its narrative speaks to us in our modern lives.

Esther's story is indeed one of courage, resilience, and unwavering faith in the face of adversity. As we delve into her experiences, we are reminded of the power of trusting in God's providence, even in the most challenging of circumstances. Just as Esther recognized the gravity of her situation and took action, may we, too, find the courage to stand up for what is right, recognizing that God is always with us, guiding our steps (Esther 4:14).

Through the pages of this magazine, our dedicated church members, pastors, elders, and deacons share their insights, offering a tapestry of perspectives that illuminate the richness of Esther's legacy. Beyond the exploration of Esther's narrative, "Living in Light of the Cross magazine" continues to champion the values of diversity and inclusivity.

Through heartfelt testimonials and genuine reflections from voices across our community, we celebrate the unity that faith fosters, transcending barriers of background and circumstance. As you engage with this edition, may you be inspired to reflect on the virtues of kindness, compassion, and selflessness exemplified in Esther's story. May her courage embolden you to face life's challenges with grace and resilience, recognizing the presence of God alongside you on your journey of faith.

Join us as we immerse ourselves in the story of Esther, and let "Living in Light of the Cross magazine" be your companion on the path to a life filled with purpose, love, and unwavering faith.

Teyran Main

Warmest Regards,
Editor-in-Chief Living in Light of the Cross Magazine

DOES ESTHER EVEN BELONG IN THE BIBLE?

PASTOR DAN CHRISTIAANS

Pastor Dan Christiaans grew up in London, Ontario. At 16, he attended a Christian camp called Camp Y.E.S, where he finally trusted Christ as his Saviour. He felt God's call toward ministry, so he and his wife, Tara, attended FaithWay Bible College of Canada before moving to Chatham to work at Maple City. He has since completed a bachelor's degree in Religion and a master's degree in Pastoral Counseling and is working toward a Doctor of Ministry degree, all through Liberty University. Dan and Tara have served at Maple City for 19 years. In that time, their family has grown significantly; they have been blessed with eight children and continue to serve as foster parents. Dan loves to serve the church through preaching, teaching, and working with the youth and young adults at Maple City.

Why is Esther even in the Bible? It's a fair and common question not levied against most other books in Holy Scripture. Esther is unique; it is the only book that does not mention the name of God in any form – not even once! It's a story revolving around the sinful king of a foreign nation, his beautiful queen who hid her Hebrew heritage, his evil right-hand man, and all the Israelites who chose not to return to the promised land when given the opportunity.

If I were God, I may have left those people and this story alone. This story and its inclusion in Scripture prove that God is much more gracious and merciful than I am!

Instead of leaving the Israelites to their fate, He weaves this surprising, entertaining story of poetic justice and undeserved deliverance. Originally written as an etiological story to explain and defend the festival of Purim, the story of Esther is a literary masterpiece and, more importantly, a poignant reminder that God is the sovereign King over all, even when all hope seems lost. The Spirit of God inspired and preserved this story for countless reasons; here are three:

1. Esther Proves the Power of God.

Good movies often revolve around a hero and a villain. Before the hero can save the day, the villain must appear to prevail; the more impossible the situation seems, the more amazing the deliverance by the hero in the end.

Welcome to the story of Esther. Ahasuerus (aka Artaxerxes), king of the world-conquering Medo-Persian Empire, was considered a god. His right-hand man, Haman, manipulates him into issuing an irreversible edict to annihilate all the Jews, thereby dashing earthly hope of Israel's survival. Brick after brick is stacked against the Israelites, and when the situation could not be worse and the gallows built to hang Mordecai were complete, the brilliant plan of God began to unfold. Esther, the queen, was placed in the kingdom for such a time as this; her dinner parties culminate in the king's discovery of Haman's treachery. He swiftly sentences Haman to hang on the gallows he built for Mordecai. Esther and Mordecai are celebrated and promoted. The people of Israel are empowered to defend themselves and ultimately have victory over their enemies. How? When the people of God are faced with impossible situations, they can take comfort in the fact that with God, nothing is impossible (Gen 18:14, Esther 4:14, Lk 1:27, Mt. 19:26).

2. Esther Protects the Promises of God

Why did God go to such great lengths to bring about salvation for the Jewish people who had so often rejected Him? It certainly was not because they deserved it! The people living in the city of Shushan and in the vast majority of the 127 provinces of Persia had been given the opportunity under Cyrus to return to the promised land, rebuild Jerusalem and the temple, and reinstate the worship of God; instead, they chose to live under a pagan king in an idolatrous land. Many believe God's name was left out of Esther because God's name was absent in the hearts and minds of the Jewish people at that time. Nevertheless, God saved His people because He had promised Eve a serpent crusher, Abraham, a son to bless all nations, David, an eternal King, and Isaiah, a suffering servant who would die for His people. God does not fail to keep any of His promises; He cannot and will not this time. He saved Israel because the Messiah and Saviour would be born to the seed of an Israeli. Over 500 years later, that promised snake-crushing King would suffer and die on the cross to fulfil God's ultimate promise of redemption for all those who trust in Him.

3. Esther Previews the Plan of God

The overarching story of Esther is a familiar one in the Bible: the people of God, largely due to their rebellion against Him, find themselves in terrible circumstances that they are powerless to overcome. Through a series of divinely orchestrated events, God delivers the Israelites by providing them with a hero (in this case, a heroine, Esther); however, at this point, the story of Esther gets interesting. By the end of chapter 7, it is clear that Haman has been defeated and Esther and Mordecai have been delivered; however, the Israelites are still in mortal danger. Rather than immediate and miraculous deliverance, God's plan requires the Israelites to fight the battles before them. He has provided victory, but they must still put on their armour and enter the fight to defend themselves in the power He has provided. It's impossible to read this account without considering its parallels to the Christian life.

Full and final deliverance has been provided by the finished work of Christ; however, believers are called to put on the armour of God and to fight the battles that lay before them in the power of the Spirit within them.

Esther is an amazing story—one to sit back and enjoy and one to learn from. Believers in the 21st century can read these pages and be reminded that God is still in control of their lives, that all His promises will come to fruition, and that they can face trials and temptations in the power provided to them by God, knowing full well that the final battle has already been won. Praise the Lord for so many wonderful reminders!

Andrew McCombe, originally from London, Ontario, earned his teaching degree at Liberty University, where he met his wife, Stacey. After teaching at Chatham Christian School for eight years, Andrew felt called to full-time ministry at MCBC. He is currently pursuing his Master of Divinity and has spent the last eight years serving in various ministries at MCBC. Andrew is dedicated to encouraging families to stand for truth and values growing a strong foundation in faith. He and Stacey, who have four children, cherish their time serving the MCBC community.

LITERATURE, STORIES AND GOD'S REDEMPTIVE WORK THROUGH ESTHER

PASTOR ANDREW MCCOMBE

"There was a boy called Eustace Clarence Scrubb, and he almost deserved it." These are the opening words of C.S. Lewis's masterful novel, *The Voyage of the Dawn Treader*. Eustace is an unimaginative and dreary character introduced into the Narnia drama, portrayed negatively at the novel's beginning. What is the source of Eustace's mundane nature? While Lewis mentions various reasons, it is not until page 87 that the reader is given a glimpse of the true nature of Eustace's shortcomings.

Finding himself in a dragon's cave, Lewis comments, "Most of us know what we should expect to find in a dragon's lair, but, as I said before, Eustace had read only the wrong books.

They had much to say about exports, imports, governments, and drains, but they were weak on dragons."

Eustace Clarence Scrubb's great shortcomings were rooted in the fact that he had never read proper stories, great narratives full of heroes, romance, danger, threats, evil villains, justice, unexpected plot changes, happy endings, and, yes, dragons. Great works of literature provide people with stories that encourage a love of all things good, beautiful, and virtuous. Stories are of great importance to the development of the next generation, grounding children in a heritage they can be proud of and ultimately pointing them toward a future of pursuing and submitting to Christ, the very Word made flesh.

The Book of Esther is one of the greatest pieces of literature ever written. There is much to be learned from the story of Esther, but it is not only the greatness of the story that bears significance for 21st-century Christians. Most importantly, its significance points to something far greater: God's sovereign plan of redemption and preserving His messianic lineage. Esther provides a narrative that spans from Abraham to Christ and all the way through to the establishment of Christ's church. Esther's story reveals that if Haman had succeeded in his evil intent, the Jewish people would have faced inescapable annihilation, and God's redemptive plan through Jesus Christ would have fizzled out prematurely. No Christ, atonement, or possible means of fellowship being restored between man and God.

The Gentiles would never have an opportunity to be brought into the covenant. However, God is sovereign, and His redemptive work through Christ would ultimately always come to completion, but it is a wonder to consider that the success of His work came through a sinful, flawed Jewish girl who lived some 480 years before Christ. In all of human history, God is writing a grand story of redemption that, just like Esther, we all have a role to play. Stories have been a means of passing down great narratives since creation. While we may have read all the wrong stories from childhood, the Book of Esther provides an opportunity to read one of the greatest stories ever written. I implore you to read the Book of Esther for all its worth. However, don't just read it simply for the joy of reading a good story (of which there is value), but read it understanding that as followers of Christ, the Book of Esther is not just a great story but part of our heritage in the Lord.

THE TRIUMPH OF FAITH: A STUDY OF THE BOOK OF ESTHER

JEYRAN MAIN

The Book of Esther, nestled within the Old Testament, is a captivating narrative that showcases God's providence and the triumph of faith in the face of dire circumstances. This article delves into the rich tapestry of Esther's story, emphasizing its biblical references and significance.

A Persian Setting and a Jewish Heroine

The story is set in the Persian Empire during the reign of King Ahasuerus (Xerxes I), a king who ruled from 486 to 465 B.C. The narrative begins with Queen Vashti's defiance of the king's command to appear before his guests, resulting in her dethronement (Esther 1:10-12). This event sets the stage for the rise of Esther, a Jewish orphan raised by her cousin Mordecai.

Esther's Rise to Queenship

Esther's ascent to queenship is nothing short of divine orchestration. Among the many young women brought to the king's palace, Esther finds favor in the eyes of all who see her, including the king, who crowns her queen (Esther 2:17). Despite her royal position, Esther keeps her Jewish identity secret, following Mordecai's advice (Esther 2:10).

Mordecai's Defiance and Haman's Plot

The plot thickens with Mordecai's refusal to bow to Haman, the king's highest official. This act of defiance infuriates Haman, who, learning of Mordecai's Jewish heritage, devises a plan to annihilate all Jews in the Persian Empire (Esther 3:5-6). The king, unaware of Esther's heritage, approves Haman's edict (Esther 3:10-11).

Esther's Courageous Intervention

Mordecai urges Esther to intercede with the king, highlighting that her silence could mean her own destruction (Esther 4:13-14). After three days of fasting and prayer, Esther approaches the king, risking her life. The king extends his golden scepter to her, showing his favor (Esther 5:2).

Esther invites the king and Haman to a banquet, where she plans to reveal her request.

The Reversal of Fortune

In a dramatic turn of events, the king, unable to sleep, discovers through the royal chronicles that Mordecai had previously saved his life from an assassination plot (Esther 6:1-3). The king orders Haman to honour Mordecai, intensifying Haman's humiliation (Esther 6:10-11).

During the second banquet, Esther reveals her Jewish identity and Haman's plot to annihilate her people (Esther 7:3-6). Enraged, the king orders Haman's execution on the very gallows Haman had prepared for Mordecai (Esther 7:9-10).

The Salvation of the Jews

With Haman dead, Esther and Mordecai work to counteract the deadly edict. The king grants them the authority to write a new decree, allowing the Jews to defend themselves against their enemies (Esther 8:11-12). On the appointed day, the Jews triumph over their adversaries, securing their safety (Esther 9:1-2).

The Establishment of Purim

In celebration of their deliverance, Mordecai and Esther establish the feast of Purim, a time of feasting, joy, and the giving of gifts to one another and to the poor (Esther 9:20-22). This festival is still observed by Jews today, commemorating their ancestors' salvation and God's providence.

Divine Providence and Human Agency

The Book of Esther, while not explicitly mentioning God, is a profound testament to divine providence and the faithfulness of God's people. Esther's courage, Mordecai's wisdom, and the Jews' ultimate triumph serve as enduring reminders of God's unseen hand guiding the course of history.

Through fasting, prayer, and courageous action, Esther and her people overcame insurmountable odds.

The story encourages believers to trust in God's providential care, to stand firm in their faith, and to act boldly in the face of injustice. The Book of Esther remains a powerful narrative of hope, resilience, and the unwavering faithfulness of God to His people.

Jeyran Main is a publisher, professional book editor and reviewer. As a newborn, she welcomes Jesus to her heart and dedicates her life to learning the word and spreading the gospel.

THE SINFULNESS OF MEN, THE SOVEREIGNTY OF GOD

ETHAN DAVENPORT

The book of Esther never mentions God, a peculiar thing for an entire book of the Bible. Nevertheless, just because He is not named does not mean His power cannot be clearly seen. The presence and purposes of our Lord are everywhere evident in this seventeenth book of the Old Testament. Any Christian's reading of Esther will leave them both confronted and comforted by the truth of God's sovereignty.

God's hand is working and moving even in King Ahasuerus's sinfulness at the book's beginning. We read that when Ahasuerus became intoxicated by wine, he demanded that his Queen Vashti be brought before him naked1 so that he could "show the peoples and the princes her beauty."2 Queen Vashti, however, refused. Sometime later, the king sent a decree to gather the most attractive young women in Persia, out of which he would select his next queen.

Ahasuerus eventually chose Esther as queen, as "she had won grace and favor in his sight more than all the virgins."3 What is noteworthy about these events is the ordinariness of God's providence. Esther's beauty was not random. The genetic formings that led to her physical appearance resulted from her sovereign God, who knit her together in her mother's womb, to borrow a phrase from Psalm 139.

Even in the moral muddiness of a perverted beauty contest, God's decree is alive and well. As foolish and sinful as the officials of ancient Persia were behaving, the events they contrived were actually the orchestration of our sovereign God! The Christian finds immense comfort in this truth. Our God "works all things according to the counsel of His will."4 Christian son or daughter, hear this: amid your deepest trials, your most debilitating sickness, and your most discouraging day, God is ordaining everything that befalls you for your sanctification and His glory. The power of God is not a conundrum to solve, nor a bitter medicine to swallow, but a pillow to lie on.

He, who is never mentioned in the Book of Esther, is, in fact, its main character. We learn from this story that when God is most silent, He is moving. Take heart, redeemed one, for your God is the same God who used Esther's story to rescue Israel from annihilation. Taking a step back, we must also remember that our Father ordained the most sinful event in all of history, the murder of our Lord Jesus Christ, to satisfy the demands of His justice in purchasing our redemption. "For our sake, he made him be sin who knew no sin so that in him we might become the righteousness of God."5 Salvation, although free for us, was infinitely costly for our sovereign God.

Like Esther, may we be a people who delight in God's sovereignty. While our trials are uncomfortable and often painful, God does not let one teardrop go to waste. Puritan Richard Sibbes, often called "Heavenly Doctor Sibbes," provides comfort for the Christian with these words: "Glory follows afflictions, not as the day follows the night but as the spring follows the winter; for the winter prepares the earth for the spring, so do afflictions sanctified prepare the soul for glory." May we be a church that treasures Christ and rejoices in His providence. Our God reigns.

Ethan Davenport is 18 years old. He began attending Maple City in 2021 and was baptized in 2022. He is currently completing his Bachelor of Arts at Hillsdale College in Hillsdale, Michigan.

1 - *While the text does not explicitly mention this, Jewish tradition holds this claim.*
2 - *Esther 1:11 ESV*
3 - *2:17*
4 - *Ephesians 1:11*
5 - *2 Corinthians 5:21*

For Such a Time as This

Samantha Egan

Esther answered the call. This story has been told and retold for thousands of years with its unforeseeable but satisfying outcome.

The aforementioned question is one, I believe, that you and I, living our much more mundane lives, ought still to ask ourselves. It's quite unlikely any of us will be called to save our people from lawful extermination, but we were born for such a time as this, and we have been given the opportunity to partake in what God is doing. On any given day, there are countless demands on our time, attention, and action. Over the past several years, the voices seem to have increased in volume and grown in number. It is not without keen intentionality that we find the space and quiet to ask ourselves that question, let alone listen to the only voice truly worthy of our ear. The voice that I need to hear most desperately is the one I have to seek. It does not force itself upon me.

In the middle of chapter four, we find a verse in which Uncle Mordecai urges his niece, Esther, to do the hard thing. His directive for her is simple: petition the King to save the Jews. If we were to rate verses in popularity, this verse would land pretty high on the charts. "Yet who knows whether you have come to the kingdom for such a time as this?" (Esther 4:14). Pretty inspiring, isn't it? But it's not placed there in the middle of a motivational speech. Just prior to this question, he reminds her of her undesirable destiny if she doesn't use her platform to do something about the impending death of her people. He also mentions, with confidence, that if not through her, protection would come another way. One thing he is sure of: Jewish deliverance.

Samantha trusted Christ at the young age of eleven. She has attended Maple City for thirteen years and is thankful to call this place home. She and her husband, Justin, have five children. Her deepest desire is to raise those children to know and love the Saviour and to be vessels used by Him.

It is found in the pages of a Holy Book or in the quiet promptings of the Holy Spirit. It is the voice of the Creator God. It is never-changing, omnipresent, and all-powerful.

So what do we do during such a time as this? We need to love people and stand up for those who cannot stand up for themselves. We need to walk so closely to the Saviour and pray that our eyes see others the way He does. We need to pursue the truth to stand confidently on a sure and unshakeable foundation. We need to show our children how to live a life for the Only One Worthy. We need to share the Good News boldly. We need to talk to Jesus.

Throughout the story of Esther, we see so beautifully the thread of God's providence. God would save His people, and He allowed Esther to be a part of the salvation plan in His goodness and in response to her obedience. How glorious it is to know that He has not changed. He is still holding the pen, writing the story of humankind. He has already won, and He invites us to be joint heirs in that victory. One day, we will worship together with every tongue and tribe. What a day that will be.

Christians, let's add to that chorus by telling and showing others the love Jesus demonstrated on the cross and the love whispered throughout the pages of His Word. Needed now, as much as ever, for such a time as this.

My story
Farmer Thomas Olsen

The year was 1969. The war in Vietnam had been in the news for 14 years. It was dubbed the unwinnable war by the liberal press. It was a difficult and unsettling time in American history. The young people were disillusioned and upset, being drafted into this senseless war that no one wanted except the military and industrial complex of the deep state. Young people rebelled, escaping reality by diving into psychedelic drugs, sexual immorality, and Rock 'n' Roll. The hippie movement was born—long hair, sandals, and rebellion against all forms of authority.

1969 was the year of the music festival in Woodstock, N.Y. Hippies from all across North America came to listen to musicians like Jimi Hendrix, Janis Joplin, and bands like The Who, Jefferson Airplane, The Grateful Dead,

Crosby, Stills, Nash & Young, etc. Perhaps the song that profoundly represented the times was performed by Country Joe and the Fish. It went like this: "1, 2, 3, what are we fighting for? I don't know, and I don't give a xxxx. The next stop is Vietnam 5, 6, 7; open the pearly gates; there ain't no time to wonder why Yippie, we're all gonna die."

In the same year, 1969, in Southern California, a hippie named Lonnie Frisbee was hitching rides to anywhere in CA with the sole purpose of witnessing to the driver about his saviour Jesus Christ. He would providentially connect to a preacher named Chuck Smith, and the "Jesus Revolution" began.

Where was I in '69? Well, I got my driver's license. I was a part of the baby boomer generation. It soon became apparent that not all the boys on the farm would end up farming. I was the only one interested in our family, but

Forgive me. Would you enter my life and redeem me? Would you sit on the throne of my heart and direct my ways and be my God?"

When I yielded myself to the Lord, the Spirit of God entered my being, and the crushing weight of sin was lifted. I knew I was born again. That little country church is still there. It stands as a memorial for me. It was nighttime, July 7, 1970, under that day-night light, that I gave my life to Jesus Christ.

The revival that swept that church 55 years ago is now a memory for most of us. Some of us fell away, some became preoccupied with life's challenges, but some remained faithful to the church. For me, that was the night everything changed. I now had purpose and direction for my life.

Now, I know that my testimony is not riveting or dramatic, but what happened the next year may prove more interesting.

In the spring of 1971, I ended up in a diagnostic hospital in Michigan for ten days, being examined by all the specialists. When I came home, the doctors gave me five years to live.

To be continued...

that dream was crushed when Dad took a job in business and sold the farm equipment. We always went to church, but I was introverted, scared of girls, without purpose or direction or knowing where the future would take me.

That year, a student minister came to our little country church. He was a product of the Jesus movement and went on to share the gospel of Jesus Christ individually with everyone in the church. My time for a visit was fast approaching. I was aware of the stir he created among the Youth Group. At the same time, I was watching a Billy Graham crusade on mainstream television (they did that back then).

The pressure was mounting, conviction became unbearable, and I knew I needed to decide. One night, I was driving aimlessly around and found myself at that little country church. I parked the car under the day-night lights and started praying.

It went something like this: "Lord, I want to be a Christian. Amen." Not good enough. I tried again. "Lord, I know I'm a sinner. Forgive my sins. I claim the blood of Jesus. Amen." I was holding back. I wanted to live and do my own thing, and the Lord knew it. You cannot con the Lord. Finally, I said: "Lord, I am a sinner.

Just a farmer

IS THAT YOU GOD? *PAUL VAN KESTEREN*

The Book of Esther is, among other things, about seizing the moment. Pithy phrases like "no time like the present," "don't put off till tomorrow what you can do today," and "a stitch in time saves nine" embody the wisdom learned through hard knocks. Even as we contemplate this concept, we often tend to turn and demand a little time to think it over. "Now" is often harsh, offering small comfort and more work. For some, its demand is a call to get the job done and over with. A few see the imperative as insight becoming action, which saves the day.

As we consider these ideas, we find Esther sitting with her beloved guardian, her uncle Mordecai. His character has endeared him to this young girl, who trusts him implicitly. He has visited the palace daily to watch over her well-being silently. During that time, his behavior has saved the King's life but enraged the next in command. Not bowing to Haman had unleashed fury not only on Mordecai but also on the entire Jewish race. Now, Mordecai is asking Esther to intervene and reveal to the King the plight of the Jewish people. Esther is terrified, not wanting to enrage the King and incur a worse judgment on herself than her predecessor, Queen Vashti.

Waiting for the best moment is never easy, and this seems how Esther felt when asked to act. She thought this was probably not the right time. "All the king's servants and the people of the king's provinces know that if any man or woman goes to the king inside the inner court without being called, there is but one law – to be put to death, except the one to whom the king holds out the golden sceptre so that he may live. But as for me, I have not been called to come into the king these thirty days." (Esther 4:11). But her encourager pushed her farther, to go beyond herself.

At this moment, the most important words spoken in this story are put before Esther. Uncle Mordecai, filled with anguish at what he must say to his little princess, poses the question which ultimately controls the entire story: "...and who knows whether you have not come into the kingdom for such a time as this?"

Now, Esther springs into action and cautiously moves toward a duty to her people and her uncle. Nothing else matters but that she does the right thing. Now, she is empowered to be willing to lose her own life for what is right. Now!

In the same way, our encourager nudges us, and we know our encourager is God. Now, we must consider our own lives in view of this young girl's courage and examine the "thoughts and intents" of our calling. Do we rise to the occasion of God's soft voice telling us we are needed in some way to make a difference? The Holy Spirit was promised to all who believe to lead us into "all righteousness." We must come to believe that the small voice we hear is God's.

From the tool box of Paul Van Kesteren

MY LIFE WITH JESUS JENNIE MARSHALL

Trying to sum up my life to write this testimony wasn't easy. My life has been one giant mess of bad habits, angry lashouts, tears, selfishness, depression, and trying to run away from it all. I have been back and forth with God my entire life, and God never left me once.

Ever since I can remember, I believed in Jesus. I grew up in a Christian home and was so in love with Jesus as a little girl. As I grew older, my excitement for Him slowly faded, but throughout the rest of my life, I had His voice in the back of my head.

Becoming friends with the wrong crowd at a young age is when my life started down a long, winding path that ultimately led to nothing. I always felt different from my friends and felt convicted doing things that we did, but I wanted so desperately to fit in. My first relationship was built on drugs. I was high on different drugs almost every day in high school, and the weekends were always one big bender.

I got addicted to pills for a while, and I got to the point that I had to ask my family for help. I went to stay with my sisters here in Chatham to detox, and I remember drawing closer to God during that time and how much love everyone surrounded me with. I went back to school, relapsed, and got involved in a much older crowd, continuing on a downward spiral.

Another terrible relationship left me questioning if I was good enough. Coming out of that relationship, I truly believed I would never be loved.

I continued seeking everything BUT God to feel good, and many years later, I had enough, so I ran away out West with no plan. A fresh start, I thought, would change everything, and it felt like it did for a moment. I prayed to God countless times on that trip to help me, and I didn't even know what I wanted help with; I was so lost. I just wanted to feel okay.

The friends I made out West were such a good change compared to the ones I had back home. I remember feeling I was finally becoming someone I always wanted to be. I was still missing something. I met a guy named Charlie shortly after moving to B.C., and he showed me the love I had never thought I deserved all those years- a love I had never thought existed. I thank God daily for the gift of Charlie's love, although I know I have had that love all along. God's love is what I was searching for.

When COVID happened, I started turning back to God, and I was fearful of the unknown. During that time, I tried to relearn things I was taught as a kid, but I didn't know how. Charlie passed away unexpectedly in 2021, and nothing was the same ever again. His death hit me really hard, and alcohol was the very first thing I turned to. I screamed to God and cried and cried out. It was like I was finally at the point where I wanted to be, but He took it all away in the blink of an eye. I cried to Him day and night, and it felt like He had never heard me.

The months that followed were filled with drinking, and blacking out became a regular thing.

But, during that time, I began to get to know God unlike I never had in my entire life. I had started to read the Word seriously for the first time, and I was eager to know Him more and more, but I was still not living for Him. Then, I ran away further to the Yukon. A fresh start again, and I continued to read the Bible more and more in between copious amounts of alcohol and blackouts. I was isolated in a small cabin surrounded by nothing but wilderness. There was lots of space to scream and cry to God there. I kept yelling at Him to help me figure out what was happening. One night before I blacked out, I screamed at Him in frustration and anger about how lost I was, and I threw my devotional against the wall. When I went to pick it up, it was open to a page with the verse in Psalm 139: "Where can I go from Your Spirit? Where can I flee from Your presence? If I go up to the heavens, You are there; if I make my bed in the depths, You are there. If I rise on the wings of the dawn, if I settle on the far side of the sea, even there, Your hand will guide me. Your right hand will hold me fast." It hit me, and I had been running from Him my whole life. I was hiding from Him, trying to fix everything myself. There was nowhere I could go where He wouldn't be. No matter how hard I tried, He was with me in every trial I faced.

After that, I decided to come back to Chatham to get sober and get closer to God. God kept bringing me back to this place in tough times, and these people were always here with wide open arms, loving me for me just as God always did. I continued to stumble more times than I'd wish, and one night, when I was lying on the ground in my own vomit, I swore it was my last time. I still struggle, but it feels different. I started seeking Him daily, and He started changing me.

It's been slow, but He has been so good to walk with, He has shown me so much grace, He is surrounding me with people to keep me close to God, and I trust His plan is bigger and better than mine ever was. I'm grateful for my past; as hard as it may be, I can finally start seeing the joy in suffering.

Romans 5 says, "We rejoice in our sufferings knowing that suffering produces endurance, endurance produces character, and character produces hope. I have no hope in myself. I have surrendered everything to Him, and I want people to know He hasn't just helped me through these trials on earth, but He died on the cross for my sins, and He saved my soul for eternity.

Jennie Marshall grew up near St. Thomas, Ontario. She has always loved to travel; at age 23, she packed her car and moved west to live in British Columbia. After a few years there and another in Whitehorse, Yukon, Jennie moved back to Ontario in 2022. Jennie is a free spirit - she loves adventure, the outdoors, and anything that poses a challenge. She was baptized at Maple City in March 2024 and is serving in various ministries at the church. She loves Jesus and lives by J. R. Tolkien's words, "not all who wander are lost."

The God-Breathed Scripture ... Even When It Doesn't Seem As Such

Trent Kenney

For those in our church who have been journeying through Pastor Dan Christiaan's series on Sunday mornings at Maple City Baptist Church, we have been enhancing our understanding of the biblical book of Esther. It may now be well known to us that the book of Esther is somewhat "secular," and that it possesses a unique quality unlike any other books of Scripture – it does not mention God by name, not even once.

With this poignancy in mind, the question that naturally arises within us might be, "What then is this book, which does not even mention God, doing in the Bible at all?" After all, should we not expect that the Bible always mentions God and highlights direct moral instruction? Why does there seem to be no explicit teachings, whether in exhortation, benedictions, parables, sarcasm, rhetoric, etc.? Why does this book appear to be merely a narrative or historical account at best?

I believe that following the hermeneutical method/law helps with our approach to understanding how our Lord God has led the authorship of this part of Scripture. And it begins with understanding the original context:

Persia was a "secular" Empire.

The book of Esther's context is the early Achaemenid (Persian Empire). While King Xerxes held the throne at the time of Esther, under the successor King Artaxerxes, the dominant religion of the Persian Empire would then be Zoroastrianism.

However, with the Persian Empire being

segregated into provinces called "satraps" (or satrapies), the empire allowed various cultures and religious practices to be embraced within or for individuals not even to practice any of them. There was freedom for the people in the satraps of the Persian Empire to choose and adhere to religious practices of their choice (or none), and it was not decreed mandatory for them to follow the state religion. For this reason, we see the Jews living in the satraps of Persia.

Even though not mentioned, the Lord is Sovereign.

All we can do is speculate and have faith in the Lord, knowing that there was a reason, inspired by the Spirit, to exclude mentioning God by name in the Book of Esther. It is our speculation that this was possibly intentional by the human author and ultimately led by the Spirit as such. We see how Queen Esther and others were led to protect the Jewish people. God is working even when not explicitly mentioned or realized.

We must remember that the Book of Esther is canonically Spirit-led Scripture.

"All Scripture is God-breathed and is useful for teaching, rebuking, correcting, and training in righteousness, so that the servant of God may be thoroughly equipped for every good work." (2 Timothy 3:16-17, NIV)

Trent Kenney has been attending Maple City Baptist Church since November 2023 with his wife, Samantha, and young son, Ezra. They had previously resided in Huntsville, ON. A graduate of Heritage College & Seminary (Cambridge, ON) and with an education in Creative Writing (Fleming College), he has always enjoyed writing. His serious endeavor of writing came when he felt led to write faith-based articles after his position as Youth & Children's Ministries Director/Pastor with Minden Bible Church (Minden, ON). While in post-secondary education and working simultaneously, he served in this church and found great enjoyment in crafting lessons and teaching in these ministries. The principles of this seemed to naturally carry into writing articles & poems thereafter.

Trent writes on the Medium platform and is also an editor for Koinonia Publication (via Medium). He has also had an article published in LOVE IS MOVING magazine.

He has had various employment experiences, including Warehouse Manager for Mark's (Canadian Tire Corp.), residential Carpenter for various carpentry crews in Muskoka, ON, Service Advisor for Hyundai Canada, grocery clerk for Foodland (Callander Foodland, Callander, ON), splitting firewood for a firewood business in Minden, ON, etc.

Trent currently works here in Chatham in the Service department for Hyundai of Chatham. He has been with Hyundai Canada for the last couple of years.

The Lessons I've Learned

Effie Gabriel

Augustine says, "When you praise, you pray twice." That quote has been a constant in my life. I was 30 years old when I finally surrendered my life to Jesus. Looking back, I remember the people God used as beacons of light as I struggled in the darkness of unbelief. I remember Mrs. Deeks, my 3rd-grade school teacher, who read the Bible to us every morning. I remember Mrs. Young, our neighbor, who watched TV evangelists with me every Sunday throughout my teens.

And I remember my sister Olga, who is now with the Lord. She was able to articulate the importance of being born again in a way that convinced me that He is the only way to achieve true peace.

When I was first saved, I was a hot mess, as you can imagine.

Everything in life was overwhelming. As I would talk to my pastor, Brother John Williams, I would tell him all my woes, and his answer to me was always the same. He would tell me, "Go home, praise the Lord, sister." I would do just that. Oddly enough, the hurdles of life became more accessible to jump over. I thought my life was on the fast track towards true contentment. I was saved. My eternity was secure. My husband and children were serving the Lord. We had a great church community, and everything was wonderfully falling into place.

That is, until the unthinkable happened. My marriage broke up. How did that happen? What now?

The pain was unbearable.

I couldn't focus when I read the Bible.

The words on the pages were just words. Nothing was getting through, or so I thought. Then I remembered my pastor's advice: "Go home, praise the Lord, sister." So I did. What did I learn? I learned that when I surrendered my life to Jesus, the Spirit of the living God came and dwelt with me. When I was born again, I didn't have to do things alone. He (the Holy Spirit of God) would gently remind me how to walk with Him through life's dark valleys.

Trials or dark valleys are God's way of perfecting me. But since He gave me a will of my own, I had to decide if I wanted to escape the pain or embrace Him until the lesson was learned. I decided I wanted to do it His way.

When I was angry with people who had wronged me, I had to depend on God to take the root of bitterness from my heart. And He did.

I depended on Him to supply all our needs when finances were extremely tight. And He did.

I was a single mother raising two teenage boys. At times, I needed Him to intervene and be the father they needed, and He was.

Psalm 46:10 says, "Be still, and know that I am God."

I started this by quoting Augustine: "When you praise, you pray twice."

In my time of despair, I would often start praising Him for relief from my trials, but if I continued singing, I slowly turned that praise and worship not for what He could do but simply because He was worthy.

He is God, and He is faithful. I am His, and He is mine. God is in control of my life, and I can trust Him.

That means all is well with my soul. Every day is a blessing with God!

He is the source of my existence. He is my Savior. If you don't know this incredible Savior, call out to Him.

Effie Gabriel has been attending MCBC since 2018

www.ingramcontent.com/pod-product-compliance
Lightning Source LLC
Chambersburg PA
CBHW041531120626
46551CB00018B/2660